Did You Know?

LEEDS

A MISCELLANY

Compiled by Julia Skinner

With particular reference to the work of Clive Hardy

THE FRANCIS FRITH COLLECTION

www.francisfrith.com

Based on a book first published in the United Kingdom in 2006 by The Francis Frith Collection®

This edition published exclusively for Identity Books in 2010 ISBN 978-1-84589-384-2

British Library Cataloguing in Publication Data

Did You Know? Leeds - A Miscellany
Compiled by Julia Skinner
With particular reference to the work of Clive Hardy

The Francis Frith Collection
Frith's Barn, Teffont,
Salisbury, Wiltshire SP3 5QP
Tel: +44 (0) 1722 716 376
Email: info@francisfrith.co.uk
www.francisfrith.com

Printed and bound in Malaysia

Front Cover: **LEEDS, BOAR LANE c1965** L28148p

The colour-tinting is for illustrative purposes only, and is not intended to be historically accurate

CONTENTS

INTRODUCTION

The middle part of Yorkshire, the old West Riding, was the powerhouse for the industrialisation of woollen and textile manufacturing. A ready supply of sheep in the upper dales, and an ingenuity in its people for inventing looms and spinning machines, meant that the West Riding was at the forefront of a global trade in textiles. Towns such as Leeds, Bradford, Halifax and Huddersfield grasped the opportunities to trade in wool, and developed along the fast-flowing rivers which originally gave power to their mills. The combination of the factory system and the application of steam power led to the concentration of textile production in a handful of towns, including Leeds. Much of the vast wealth created was then invested in the splendid civic buildings which abound in the area.

Leeds was originally a 'wool' town, but by the mid 19th century factories in the area moved into the field of ready-made clothing and tailoring, and by the beginning of the 20th century Leeds was the world centre for that trade. By 1921 Montague Burton's mill was the largest clothing manufactory in the world. Bobbins and shuttles still fly at Armley Mills Industrial Museum, vividly illustrating the working lives of many Leeds people in the city's heyday. Other industries in the city have included the manufacture of a large variety of commodities, ranging from footwear to ferro-concrete construction.

Leeds Station is the busiest in the UK, outside London. The A1(M), M1 and M62 all intersect at Leeds, making it the principal northern hub of the motorway network. These excellent transport links have been a significant factor contributing to the growth of Leeds, and the city has become a centre for distribution. The service sector is now an important part of the Leeds economy, dominating over the city's manufacturing industries.

Also important is the 'super highway' of modern computer technology - over 33% of the UK's internet traffic goes through Leeds, making it the UK's largest internet city.

Modern-day Leeds is a bustling, forward-looking city with much new development, many interesting modern buildings such as K2 and Prince's Exchange, and the exciting Millennium Square. Leeds came top in a poll by The Independent newspaper to find the best place in Britain to live in 2004/5.

The story of Leeds is full of fascinating characters and events, of which this book can only provide a brief glimpse.

THE PARKINSON BUILDING c1960 L28099

LOCAL DIALECT WORDS AND PHRASES

An inhabitant of Leeds is traditionally known as a Loiner, a term derived from the word 'Loin' for a roll of cloth, and thus a reference to Leeds as a centre of the cloth trade.

'Ah'm sad flayed' - I'm a bit stupid.

'Get agate then' - get on with it.

'Baht' - without.

'Moudiwarp' - a mole.

'Fuzzock' - a donkey.

'Leit green' - crafty, cunning.

'Laike' - play.

The name 'Leeds' is believed to come from 'Leodis', which was a name recorded in Anglo-Saxon sources.

HAUNTED LEEDS

Temple Newsam is said to be haunted by a number of ghosts. The Blue Lady is the best known, and is traditionally believed to be the ghost of Mary Ingram, whose portrait hangs above the fireplace in the Green Damask Room. She was robbed by a highwayman while returning home by carriage one night, and afterwards became obsessed with hiding her possessions. The ghost of the Blue Lady has been reported apparently frantically searching for something, presumably her lost belongings. Another ghost, the White Lady, is said to be that of Lady Jane Dudley, a young lady who fell in love with Lord Darnley, later the husband of Mary, Queen of Scots. Lord Darnley was born at Temple Newsam. Lady Jane's love for Lord Darnley was not reciprocated, and she hanged herself when she heard of his betrothal to the queen. Other ghosts at Temple Newsam are said to be those of a monk, a Knight Templar and a small boy. There are also a number of unexplained phenomena such as the sensation of something pushing past people on the stairs, a mysterious 'misty form', and the sounds of screaming coming from the South Wing.

The City Varieties Theatre is said to be haunted late at night by the ghost of a mysterious piano player.

An old folklore belief in the Leeds area was that the souls of babies who died before they were baptised would return to haunt their parents, in the shape of devil dogs known as Gabble Retchets.

The old gatehouse of Kirkstall Abbey, now the Abbey House Museum, is believed to be haunted by the ghost of a former abbot.

The Bridewell - a small prison beneath the town hall - is said to be haunted by the ghost of Charlie Peace, a violent thief and double murderer who was held there before his trial and execution at Armely Prison in 1879.

LEEDS MISCELLANY

The statue seen in photograph L28015, opposite, is of Edward of Woodstock, better known as the Black Prince on account of his black armour. The son of Edward III, he was already a seasoned warrior at the age of 16, and made his name at the battle of Crécy in 1346. He commanded the king's forces at the battle of Poitiers in 1356, at which the French king was captured. The statue, by the local sculptor Thomas Brock, was commissioned by the Lord Mayor, Thomas Walter Harding, to celebrate Leeds achieving city status in 1893, although it was to be another ten years before it was unveiled. Harding, who was a rich industrialist, paid for the statue and decided that it should portray the Black Prince, whose virtues he admired, although the prince had no connection with Leeds.

By the late 14th century the trade guilds at York and Beverley were so over-regulated and over-taxed with guild levies that they were unable to compete against the challenge of cheaper textiles from towns such as Leeds, Halifax and Wakefield, where production costs were lower. By the early 16th century Leeds had emerged as the leading centre in Yorkshire for the trade in woollen cloths, and the town was expanding; the population in 1560 was about 3,000, if the outlying hamlets of Woodhouse, Buslingthorpe, Potternewton and Knowsthorpe are taken into consideration, and there were houses on both sides of Briggate as far as the Headrow, and others beyond Timble Bridge over Sheepscar Beck.

THE BLACK PRINCE STATUE
c1955 L28015

BINGLEY, FIVE RISE LOCKS c1900 B98501

The Leeds & Liverpool Canal was sanctioned in 1770. At 127 miles in length, excluding branches, the canal was the longest in Britain. The first section, Bingley to Skipton, was opened by 1773 and in 1777 the sections from Aire and Calder at Leeds to Gargrave, and from Wigan to Liverpool were open for traffic. Then the money ran out. In 1790 a new Act allowed funds to be raised for the construction of the middle section, but following the outbreak of war with France the funding slowed down and it was not until 1816 that the canal was open throughout. One of the problems suffered by the Leeds & Liverpool was a lack of adequate water supplies. In long dry summers some sections had to be closed for weeks at a time, and despite the heavy payloads capable of being carried, carriers were forced to seek a reliable alternative.

The five rise locks at Bingley (above) are part of the Leeds & Liverpool Canal, and are one of the wonders of the waterway system. They are known as staircase locks, because the top gate of each chamber is also the bottom one of the next: there is no water between the two.

Just four miles from Leeds city centre is Temple Newsam, a grand Jacobean house which is now an important museum and art gallery. It is often dubbed 'The Hampton Court of the North'. Amongst the treasures to be found there is a fine collection of Leeds Pottery (see page 27).

During the First World War, Leeds contributed over 90,000 men to the forces, of whom 9,640 were killed in action. The greatest single loss on one day occurred on 1 July 1916 during the Somme offensive, when the Leeds Pals suffered appalling casualties and were all but wiped out.

THE WAR MEMORIAL AND THE HEADROW c1955 L28005

The 17th-century side-saddle traveller Celia Fiennes visited Leeds in 1698, and described it as 'a large town, severall large streetes cleane and well pitch'd and good houses all built of stone, some have good gardens and steps up to their houses and walls before them; this is esteemed the wealthiest town of its bigness in the Country. Its manufacture is the woollen cloth the Yorkshire Cloth in which they are all employ'd and are esteemed very rich and very proud … they have provision soe plentiful that they may live with very little expense and get much variety; here if one calls for a tankard of ale which is allwayes a groate – it's the only dear thing all over Yorkshire, their ale is very strong – but for paying this groat for your ale you may have a slice of meate either hotte or cold according to the time of day you call, or else butter and cheese gratis into the bargaine, this was a general custom in most parts of Yorkshire but now they have almost changed it, and tho' they still retaine the great price for the ale yet make Strangers pay for their meate, and some places at great rates, notwithstanding how cheape they have all their provision; there is still this custome on a Market day at Leeds the sign of the Bush just by the bridge, any body that will goe and call for one tanckard of ale and a pinte of wine and pay for these only, shall be set to a table to eate with 2 or 3 dishes of good meate and a dish of sweetmeats after; had I known this and the day which was their Market, I would have come then but I happened to come a day after the Market, however I did only pay for 3 tankards of ale and what I eat and my servants was gratis.'

BRIGGATE c1955 L28010

HEADINGLEY, THE CRICKET GROUND PAVILION 1897 39099

Photograph 39099, above, shows the home of Yorkshire County Cricket Club at Headingley. Originally a part of the Cardigan Fields estate, Headingley was put on the market in 1888 and Lot 17A was purchased by a group of businessmen with an enthusiasm for sports. This was to become the home of the Leeds Cricket, Football and Athletic Company. The very first cricket match played here in 1890 was between Leeds and Scarborough. Also, in the same year a North of England XI entertained the Australian team. Yorkshire County matches transferred to the ground from the previous county pitch at Sheffield - in the first Yorkshire cricket game in 1891, the home team lost to Derbyshire by 45 runs. Test cricket came in 1899, and rugby was first played here in 1895 by Leeds FC, one of the 20 original clubs that formed the Rugby League.

When the Town Hall was opened by Queen Victoria in 1858 the streets were lined with palm trees and triumphal arches. The Town Hall with its magnificent many-pillared clock tower was designed by the Hull architect Cuthbert Broderick, who also designed the Corn Exchange, and has been described as one of the best examples of the Classical Revival style in England. Built between 1853 and 1858, this sumptuous public building was deliberately ambitious in scale, its dignified and spectacular classical lines symbolising the reputation of Leeds as the leading city of the West Riding.

THE TOWN HALL 1894 34765

Kirkstall Abbey played a part in the industrial development of Leeds, for it was here that iron forging first began in the district. The abbey was founded in 1152 as a daughter house of Fountains. Building work was completed by 1175, and iron forging began in 1200. Kirkstall is one of the finest and most complete examples of early Cistercian architecture in Britain. The main entrance to the abbey church was through the imposing porch seen in photograph 7411, opposite, enriched with capitals with scalloped details; the original circular window above was replaced by the two round-arched windows in the late 15th century. After the Dissolution the abbey was left a ruin, and many of its stones were eventually carted off and used to widen the old Leeds Bridge. Even so, the chapter house, cloisters and abbot's lodging are still impressive. The gatehouse was converted to a private house and is now the Abbey House Museum, showing life in Leeds in the 19th century.

The great industrial city of Leeds that we know today grew from much humbler beginnings. When William the Conqueror's survey of his new land and wealth, the Domesday Book, was compiled in 1086, Leeds was little more than a village huddled between the river and what is now Kirkgate. 35 families were listed as living there, with a priest, a church and a mill - the latter doing well enough to be worth four shillings a year.

By 1830 Leeds was one of the busiest stagecoaching interchanges in the provinces, with well over 100 daily scheduled services leaving the coaching inns in Briggate. In 1835 coaching was at its peak with around 3,300 stagecoaches and over 700 mail coaches operating daily scheduled services thoughout the country.

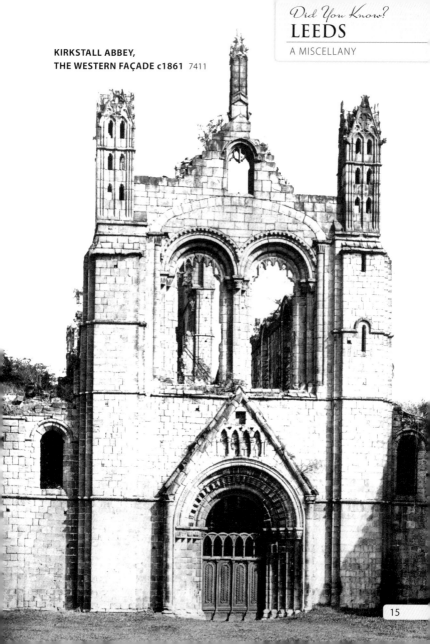

**KIRKSTALL ABBEY,
THE WESTERN FAÇADE c1861** 7411

DUNCAN STREET c1955 L28011

The view above shows the junction of Boar Lane and Briggate, looking towards the Corn Exchange. One of the highlights of shopping along Briggate was the glass-roofed arcades, such as the Queen's and the County. In earlier days Briggate was where the merchants and clothiers assembled to buy and sell cloth; the street had many small inns for the market customers, built on plots in yards behind the street. The Corn Exchange is one of the finest Victorian structures in the city. Built by Cuthbert Broderick in 1862, its magnificent domed glass roof, 75ft high, once threw light on market dealings below; today a variety of designer shops are housed here.

Leeds is in the old West Riding of Yorkshire. It was Viking Danes who first divided the huge county of Yorkshire into the ridings, or 'thridings' - thirds - and they became the North, East and West Ridings before local government reorganisation in 1974.

In Leeds and the surrounding villages, cloth manufacture seems to have been underway on a small scale by the 12th century, almost certainly influenced by the close proximity of the Cistercian abbey of Kirkstall. This was endowed by Henry de Lacy in thanks to the Blessed Virgin, after his recovery from a serious illness. Kirkstall, like the great Cistercian abbeys of Fountains, Rievaulx and Jervaulx, grew rich through keeping huge flocks of sheep for wool. In the 12th century most of the wool was sold for weaving in Flanders and Northern Italy, though there was a considerable amount of weaving done at both York and later Beverley, with Leeds, Wakefield, Whitby and Selby the poor relations.

KIRKSTALL ABBEY 1891 28286

BRIGGATE c1951 L28012

On the left of photograph L28012, above, is the oldest shop in
Leeds, dating from 1613, undergoing some maintenance at the
time this view was taken. Further along the street is The Empire
Theatre. This view of the street reveals a complex picture of
turreted and pedimented Victorian buildings in a wide range of
styles.

By 1612 the population of Leeds had doubled, partly due to people
migrating to the town in search of work. Building development now
extended along Kirkgate, Boar Lane, Vicar Lane and Swinegate; an
ever-growing mixture of housing and workshops sprung up, as the
position of Leeds within the textile industry continued to strengthen.
The town was no longer simply engaged in manufacturing, but had
become the leading finishing centre in the West Riding for cropping,
dyeing and dressing. Leeds merchants traded aggressively both at
home and abroad, securing markets previously dominated by the
merchants of York, Beverley and Hull.

Main-line railways came to Leeds in 1834 with the opening of the Leeds & Selby line. By 1840 the Leeds & Selby line had been extended to Hull and a direct rail link with the Midlands had been opened, thanks to the North Midland Railway line to Derby, where there was an end-on connection with the Derby & Birmingham. At this time the Leeds & Manchester Railway did not run directly into town but connected with the North Midland at Normanton. In 1846 the Leeds & Bradford line opened, followed in 1848 by the London & North Western line. In 1849 Headingley and Horsforth were linked by rail to Leeds with the opening of the Leeds Northern to Harrogate. On the eve of the railway amalgamations of 1 January 1923, Leeds was at the centre of a comprehensive railway network and served by five railway companies: the London & North Western, the Midland, the North Eastern, the Lancashire & Yorkshire, and the Great Northern. There were passenger stations at Wellington Street, Leeds Central and Leeds New. Goods facilities were at Wellington Street, Cardigan Road, Hunslet Lane and Central.

BRIGGATE c1965 L28142

During the Civil War, Sir William Savile entered Leeds at the head of a Royalist force of 500 horsemen and 1,500 foot soldiers in January 1643. He set about fortifying the town: artillery was sited to cover Briggate, earthworks were thrown up at the north end of Leeds Bridge and a trench was dug around the town perimeter to the banks of the Aire. On 23rd January, Sir Thomas Fairfax at the head of a Parliamentarian force of 3,000 men crossed the Aire at Apperley Bridge and halted on Woodhouse Moor. Sir Thomas followed the rules of engagement of the day by offering Sir William terms. Sir William declined, and the assault began at around 2pm. Within two hours the Parliamentarians had broken through the defences and the battle was soon over. Though Sir William escaped, 500 of his men were taken prisoner, but were allowed to go free after promising to take no further part in the war, as was the custom.

By 1600 Leeds had established itself as the most important of all the cloth fairs in the country. Every Tuesday and Saturday, tables were set up on the bridge over the Aire at the bottom of Briggate. When the market bell tolled, the sellers would move to the tables, which they had to share, and stand in line behind their pieces. The traders entered when the bell stopped tolling. Business was done in a whisper so that other buyers and sellers could not overhear the price agreed. After a couple of hours, the bell tolled to signal the end of the market and everything was cleared away. Daniel Defoe, who visited Leeds in the 1720s, reckoned that in a morning, cloth was traded to the value of between £10,000-£20,000.

An arch commemorating the occasion of Queen Victoria's visit to Leeds in 1858 to open the Town Hall was erected in north Leeds. It was renovated in 1984 and still stands, but it is well hidden in woodland at Beckett Park in Headingley.

Recorded on the tomb of Frederick Twitchell in Leeds:

Here lie the bones of Lazy Fred,
Who wasted precious time in bed.
Some plaster fell down on his head,
And thanks be praised - our Freddie's dead.

To mark the millennium a new statue was planned for Leeds, to be sited on the Eastgate Roundabout, in front of the West Yorkshire Playhouse. Funding for the artwork was provided by a local trust, the Scurrah Wainwright Charity, and the Leeds Civic Trust organised a vote by the people of Leeds, to choose the subject for the work. The vote was widely publicised, and thousands of people voted for their choice from a selection of famous people who had connections with Leeds, including the Pudsey architect Benjamin LaTrobe, who designed most of the US Capitol in Washington, Isabella Ford, the radical Quaker reformer of Adel and Henry Moore OM, the great sculptor. The final choice was that the statue should commemorate a young airman who won the Victoria Cross in the Second World War, Arthur Aaron VC. Aaron graduated in architecture from Leeds University before becoming one of 23 cadets who formed the Inaugural Flight of Leeds University Air Squadron in 1941. He was awarded his pilot's wings in June 1942 and commenced active service. His plane was attacked on his 20th operational flight against Turin in 1943, when the navigator was killed and Aaron himself was mortally wounded. The crew managed to fly the seriously damaged plane to Algeria, a journey of five hours, where Aaron succeeded in landing the plane, despite his injuries. He died a few hours later, and was posthumously awarded the Distinguished Flying Medal and the Victoria Cross. The 5m-high bronze statue shows the young airman with children from the period 1950-2000 climbing up a tree; the highest and smallest child is a girl releasing the dove of peace.

ROUNDHAY PARK,
THE DRINKING FOUNTAIN c1960 R247005

Did You Know?
LEEDS
A MISCELLANY

YORKSHIRE COLLEGE 1894 34767

Yorkshire College was originally Yorkshire College of Science; it opened in 1877, and the first student was a miner. The college later became part of the Victoria University, the other colleges being at Manchester and Liverpool, when the science specialism was extended to embrace languages and history. The colleges went their separate ways in 1904, and it was out of this college that Leeds University was founded. There were originally four departments: mathematics and experimental physics, geology and mining, chemistry and textiles. The original site now nestles behind the 1951 Portland stone Parkinson building seen on page 3.

Roundhay Park was once part of a hunting estate for John of Gaunt. The land was purchased in 1803 by Thomas Nicholson, who created the two lakes and the parkland. Mansion House dates from 1826. The Mayor of Leeds, John Barran, the pioneer of mass produced clothing, bought the old Roundhay estate at auction in 1871, and then sold it at cost to the Leeds Corporation, who opened it in 1872 as the country's first municipal park. It comprised 775 acres, including woodlands, lakes and a manor house, part of which were turned into refreshment rooms. Along with Woodhouse Moor to the north, the park was considered the chief lung of the city, where for a few hours at the weekend factory workers had an opportunity to get away from the dust, grime, noise and smell of the workplace. The 33-acre lake was constructed from an old quarry.

ROUNDHAY PARK LAKE 1897 39092

ST JOHN'S CHURCH, THE INTERIOR 1897 39094

There are no medieval churches in Leeds. The church of St John the Evangelist, whose interior is seen in photograph 39094, above, was consecrated in 1634 and retains its oaken interior and a great screen which is considered to be one of the finest of its type in England. The interior of the church is also noteworthy for being in the form of two naves, rather than nave and aisle. The 17th-century box pews were irreparably damaged in the 'restoration' of the 1860s by Norman Shaw, when they were cut down. However, the beautiful old screen, with its elaborate strapwork crowns, was retained. On the left of the photograph is the two-decker pulpit and tester.

Coalmining was at one time a major industry in the Leeds area; at its height there were 102 local collieries, employing 5,000 miners, with an annual total output of 2.5 million tons.

By 1710 open-air cloth markets, such as the busy one at Leeds, were being challenged by Cloth Halls, where business could be done inside, whatever the weather. In 1711 Leeds had such a hall, in Kirkgate, for White Cloths. In 1755 a new and much larger purpose-built White Cloth Hall was opened, followed a few months later by a Mixed (Coloured) Cloth Hall. Leeds Post Office was built on the site of the Mixed Cloth Hall in 1896.

The Leeds Pottery was founded by the brothers John and Joshua Green in partnership with Richard Humble in 1770. The company was a major manufacturer of household goods in a variety of types of ceramic forms in the late 18th and early 19th centuries, the most popular being the elegant and decorative creamware - this was made from white Cornish Clay with a translucent glaze, producing a type of earthenware in a pale cream colour. By 1781 the company had been joined by William Hartley, and under the name Hartley Green & Co the company flourished, exporting its wares to Spain, Portugal, Germany, France, the Low Countries, Poland, Russia, Denmark, Italy, South America and elsewhere. The creamware became so popular that it became known as Leedsware, noted for its fine embossing and intricate openwork decoration. In the Victorian period tastes changed - the decorated style of the pottery became unfashionable, and the factory concentrated on utilitarian ware for the lower end of the market. In the 19th century the company went through several changes of ownership, and eventually closed in 1878. However, surviving moulds and clues from pattern books together with fine examples of Leeds pieces in local museums has enabled some production of creamware to the original designs to continue to this day, although it is a skilled and painstaking process. For more information about the history of Leeds Pottery see the website www.leedsware.com and visit Temple Newsam to see examples of this attractive pottery.

HEADINGLEY 1894 34773

More than half of Headingley was at one time owned by the Earl of Cardigan, and it was the enclosure of the moor at Far Headingley that had led to its development. After 1821 the village expanded as a result of the opening of several textile factories nearby. Headingley was also an attractive residential area for a growing middle class, able to escape from the polluted and overcrowded conditions of Leeds. Those who could afford to were moving to the leafier northern suburbs. Linked to Leeds by rail, horse-drawn omnibus and tram, Headingley's appeal to the middle classes declined after the 1890s, when many workers' houses were built there.

The running of the postal service in Victorian times was considered vital to the public good. The grand and impressive frontage of the Leeds Post Office, seen below, reflected the Victorian preoccupation with good communications as essential to encourage a prosperous commercial and business community. Post Offices had long opening hours, there were several postal deliveries each day, and delivery boys carried parcels to and from the city's shops and businesses. The Mixed (Coloured) Cloth Hall once stood on this site, where traders were allowed just one hour's trading per day. After its demolition the cupola from the roof tower was reused, and can still be seen on the nearby Metropole Hotel. A statue of Sir Robert Peel once stood opposite the Post Office, but it was moved to the Town Hall square in 1903, and moved again in 1937 to keep the statue of Queen Victoria company on Woodhouse Moor.

THE POST OFFICE AND REVENUE OFFICE 1897 39088

MILL WORKERS F6039

By 1775 the population of Leeds is thought to have been about 17,000, but by the time of the first census of 1801 it had rocketed to 53,000. The Industrial Revolution and the development of the factory system led to thousands of people leaving the countryside to come to Leeds in search of work, but their new working conditions would probably have been very different to what they had previously been used to: strict discipline, regular attendance, long hours and unsafe working practices contrasted with the farm work or cottage-industry conditions that many people had known before.

The imposing Italianate building of the Mechanics' Institute with its
lofty round-arched windows was designed by Cuthbert Broderick
in the late 1860s (shown in photograph L28008, below). Mechanics'
Institutes were found in most industrial towns in the 19th century,
and gave workers the chance to improve their educational and
employment prospects: they offered educational courses, backed
up with examinations, as well as evening classes and lectures. The
building later became the Civic Theatre.

COOKRIDGE STREET, THE MECHANICS' INSTITUTE c1955 L28008

31

HORSFORTH, TOWN STREET 1901 47133

Horsforth, situated at the north-western edge of Leeds, remained independent until the local government reorganisation of 1974. Along with Pudsey, Yeadon, Aireborough, Otley, Harewood, Bardsey, Linton, Wetherby, Boston Spa, Aberford, Garforth, Ledsham, Rothwell and Morley, it became a part of the City of Leeds Metropolitan District.

Yorkshire mill owners were at the forefront when it came to employing child labour in the 18th and 19th centuries. Many of these children were sent north from London workhouses. Those who ended up in the mills around Leeds were luckier than the children sent to Bradford: in Leeds they only had to work a 12-hour day, against a 13-hour day in Bradford, but in both places the children were beaten to keep them awake.

The Ivanhoe Clock in Thornton's Arcade depicts scenes from Sir
Walter Scott's 'Ivanhoe', with a moving tableau of painted wooded
figures. Robin Hood and Gurth the Swineherd strike the quarter
hours, and Friar Tuck and Richard the Lionheart strike the hours. The
clock symbolises the Leeds connection with the Knights Templar,
who feature in 'Ivanhoe': there was a preceptory of the Knights
Templar at Temple Newsom.

Trams rattle along Briggate in the view shown in photograph L28010,
on page 11. Leeds was one of the pioneers of segregated tracks,
keeping trams and other vehicles apart. The routes to Roundhay,
Belle Isle, Middleton, Temple Newsom and Lawnswood were mainly
segregated systems and, as a consequence, extremely efficient.

HORSFORTH, TOWN STREET c1960 H118032

NEW BRIGGATE c1955 L28001

At the beginning of the 20th century Leeds had four theatres, including The Grand, which is featured on the right-hand side of the above photograph. The other Leeds theatres were The Royal in Land's Lane, The Queen's in Meadow Road and The Empire Palace in Briggate.

Although Leeds became a major engineering centre in the 19th century, iron-making was always on a small scale and even in 1871 there were only two blast furnaces in the borough. There were, however, a large number of foundries, such as the Leeds Forge Co and Kirkstall Forge Co, producing all manner of castings. However, towards the end of the 19th century the production of wrought iron declined as steel gained in popularity, and most firms switched to using steel imported from Middlesbrough, Sheffield and Rotherham.

The Black Prince statue forms the centrepiece of City Square. Around the statue are four pairs of lampholders, surely among the most beautiful lampholders ever created. By Alfred Drury, they represent semi-draped girls, each holding aloft an art nouveau lamp. These 'Drury girls' date from 1899, and are symbolic of Morning and Evening. Morning, whose drapery swirls out from a morning breeze, bears a handful of fresh roses; Evening, in the wispiest outfit, stretches languorously before night falls, her eyes are already shut.

The Norman church of St John the Baptist at Adel stands in the north of Leeds (see photograph 28269, below). It was built around 1150 on the site of a Saxon church, and the south porch was added a decade later. Ancient animal symbols festoon the porch - they represent the four evangelists. The inner arch contains 40 beak heads, possibly suggesting the 40 days and nights of Christ's fast in the wilderness.

ADEL, THE CHURCH 1891 28269

THE CITY CENTRE c1965 L28135

The City Varieties Music Hall in Leeds is one of the last old-time
music halls in Britain. It became famous as the venue for the
popular television show 'The Good Old Days'. The show still
plays in Leeds, and 'whistling, shouting and similar displays
of enthusiasm (no tomato throwers please) are positively
encouraged!' Theatregoers are encouraged to wear period
fashions, and there is a prize for the best costume.

By the mid 19th century there was an enormous diversity
in the manufacturing base of Leeds. Although woollens still
dominated the scene, the flax industry employed over 9,000
workers, and other industries included rope, glass, earthenware
and paper manufacturing. Engineering also played an
important part in the development of Leeds, and Fairbairn &
Lawson manufactured flax and tow machinery, much of which
went for export.

Halfway between Leeds and Harrogate is Harewood House, one of Yorkshire's finest and stateliest of stately homes. It was designed by John Carr and Robert Adam, and the 1,000 acre parkland was created by 'Capability' Brown. The north front of the house was remodelled in 1843 by the great Victorian architect Sir Charles Barry, who with Pugin also designed the Houses of Parliament. The house contains many treasures, including an unrivalled collection of 18th-century furniture made especially for Harewood by the great furniture designer Thomas Chippendale, who was born at Otley.

The Civic Hall, shown in L28065, below, was designed by E Vincent Harris and opened with much ceremony in 1933, with temporary stands being erected for spectators. It is curious in that the façade incorporates features in two distinct traditions - the classical four-column portico and pediment, and the Wren-style slim towers. The side elevations, however, are in a more modern style. Behind and to the left are buildings of the Central Colleges.

THE CIVIC HALL, CALVERLEY STREET c1965 L28065

In the 1870s, Leeds was smoke-covered and overcrowded. Three-quarters of the population was crammed into one-eighth of the area of the borough, in some of the most appalling housing in existence. As more and more people had flocked to Leeds in search of work, cheap housing had been thrown up to accommodate them, often without any thought being given to sewage disposal or water supply. The result was that infectious diseases were often rife in working-class areas: cholera epidemics killed 700 people in 1832 and over 2,000 in 1848-49. One tourist attraction in Wellington Yard in 1872 was a midden that was 6ft deep, 6ft wide and 21ft long!

The development of Leeds into one of the leading industrial centres in the country was in part due to the development of transport and communication links, especially after the introduction of turnpiking, whereby a system of toll-roads was set up all over the country; each section was established and maintained by a group of investors, with part of the income from the tolls being used to keep the road clear and in good repair. The Leeds-to-Bradford turnpike was one of the busiest in the country, carrying large quantities of freight as well as passenger traffic. In 1778 tolls on this road amounted to £852; by 1798 the sum was £2,843 and in 1810 it had risen to £4,445.

The 11th-century village of 'Leeds' was under the lordship of Ilbert de Lacy, William the Conqueror's deputy in this region of England, and so appears to have escaped the king's wrath when he laid waste much of Yorkshire following uprisings against the new Norman rule in the northern lands in 1069-70. The people of this area were lucky: William's reprisals were deliberate and savage, and it has been estimated that one-third of the West Riding villages were destroyed. Symeon of Durham wrote of William's 'Harrying of the North', describing the devastation wrought on towns, villages and farmsteads, and of the corpses left to rot where they had fallen.

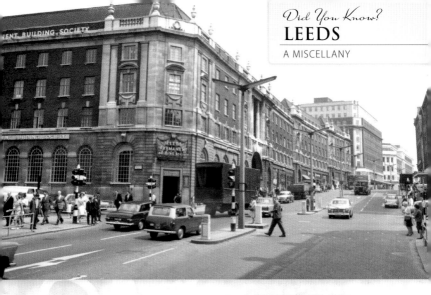

THE HEADROW c1965 L28137

In the 19th century the Leeds area became a centre for the manufacture of railway locomotives, with such firms as Todd, Kitson & Laird, Fenton, Murray & Jackson, and E B Wilson & Co. When E B Wilson & Co closed in the 1850s much of the equipment and patterns were purchased by Manning, Wardle & Co, with the result that Manning's early locomotives looked like E B Wilson's products. By the 1850s, Kitson's Airedale foundry was also turning out traction, stationary and ploughing engines for John Fowler, though Fowler eventually opened his own works. In 1860 yet another locomotive manufacturer appeared on the scene with the opening of Hudswell, Clarke & Co, followed in 1864 by the Hunslet Engine Co. The latter would be the last of the Leeds locomotive builders to remain in business, surviving into the 1990s.

The turnpike roads of the 18th century enabled scheduled daily stagecoach services to operate from Leeds to York, Hull, Sheffield, Manchester, Birmingham, Carlisle and London. In the 1750s the journey from Leeds to London took at least four days, but by the end of the 18th century turnpikes had helped to make the journey possible in just one day.

Because of an observation that there was no drinking water in Roundhay Park, the architect Thomas Ambler was commissioned to design a fountain. The result was the elegant structure seen in photograph 21003, below. It was connected to the water supply of Leeds, providing continuous refreshment through 20 taps.

THE FOUNTAIN AT ROUNDHAY PARK 1888   21003

SPORTING LEEDS

The Headingley stadium is almost certainly unique in sport. It is effectively two grounds, for both cricket and rugby, unified by a stand which has one side facing the cricket pitch and one side facing the rugby pitch. Both grounds regularly host international fixtures. The rugby ground is also home to two teams, the Leeds Rhinos Rugby League team, and the Leeds Tykes Rugby Union team.

Leeds Tykes Rugby Union Club is a relatively young club, having been formed from an amalgamation of clubs in Roundhay and Headingley. Over the years the two old clubs produced at least 40 international players, including Peter Winterbottom, who became only the second player in the sport's history to appear 50 times for England.

Since its formation as a 'super club' in 1963, City of Leeds Swimming Club has enjoyed great success in producing international medal winners. These have included Adrian Moorhouse, who won Olympic gold, Andy Astbury, who won Olympic bronze, and two World Championship winners, James Hickman and Claire Huddart. The club has won the National Club Championship on many occasions.

Rugby players moving between the two codes in deals involving large sums of money are fairly commonplace nowadays, but Leeds Rugby League Club was a long way ahead of its time when it amazed the rugby world by paying a record fee of £6,000 for Llanelli Union star Lewis Jones in 1952. The move eventually paid rich dividends when the team won its first League Championship in 1961 under Jones's captaincy.

The famous and successful Leeds United Football Club of the late 1960s and early 1970s was notable for the continuity in its playing staff. Six players from this era made over 700 appearances for the club - Jack Charlton and Billy Bremner both played on 773 occasions - and three more players made more than 500 appearances.

QUIZ QUESTIONS

Answers on page 48.

1. Which visitor to Leeds received a tankard filled with gold in 1646?

2. What were blind-backs?

3. What did 2,500 Leeds people pay 3 pennies per head to see in 1809?

4. What generous gift did Lord Brotherton make to Leeds?

5. Apart from the statue of the Black Prince, who do the four statues of famous men in City Square portray?

6. Which famous chain of High Street shops started on a market stall in Leeds in 1884?

7. A 'Drury girl', one of the art nouveau statues by Alfred Drury that can be found in Leeds, stands in Park Square surrounded by pigs. Who does she represent?

8. What name is sometimes given to Leeds as a compliment to the city's excellent shopping facilities?

9. During the Dark Ages, Leeds was in which ancient kingdom?

10. What is hidden in the depths of the lake in Roundhay Park?

RECIPE

YORKSHIRE BUN LOAF

Ingredients

275g/10oz self-raising flour

100g/4oz margarine

75g/3oz caster sugar

2 eggs, beaten

2 teaspoons marmalade

75g/3oz sultanas

75g/3oz currants

A little milk

Sift the flour into a bowl. Rub in the margarine, then stir in the sugar, eggs, marmalade, sultanas and currants. Bind to a medium stiff mixture with milk, then turn into a greased 500g/1lb loaf tin. Sprinkle the top with caster sugar and bake in a preheated moderately hot oven (190 degrees C/375 degrees F/Gas Mark 5) for 1 hour.

HORSFORTH, NEW ROAD SIDE c1965 H118094

THE HEADROW AND THE TOWN HALL c1955 L28004

RECIPE

YORKSHIRE CURD TART

The distinguishing and traditional characteristic of Yorkshire Curd
Tart is allspice (or 'clove pepper' as it was also known),
but mixed spice can be substituted for the ground allspice
if this flavour is preferred.

Ingredients

For the pastry:
115g/4oz butter, diced
225g/8oz plain flour
1 egg yolk

For the filling:
A large pinch of ground allspice

90g/3½oz soft light brown sugar
3 eggs, beaten
Grated rind and juice of 1 lemon
40g/1½oz melted butter
450g/1lb curd cheese, or
cottage cheese if curd cheese is
hard to find
75g/3oz raisins or sultanas

Preheat the oven to 190 degrees C/375 degrees F/Gas Mark 5.

To make the pastry - rub the butter into the flour until the mixture
resembles fine breadcrumbs. Stir the egg yolk into the flour mixture
with a little water to bind the dough together. Turn the dough on to
a lightly floured surface, knead lightly and form into a ball. Roll out
the pastry thinly and use to line a 20cm/8in fluted loose-bottomed
flan tin. Chill for 15 minutes.

To make the filling - mix the ground allspice or mixed spice if
preferred with the sugar, then stir in the eggs, lemon rind and juice,
butter, curd or cottage cheese and dried fruit. Pour the filling into
the chilled pastry case, then bake in the preheated oven for about
40 minutes until the pastry is cooked and the filling is lightly set and
golden brown. Serve still slightly warm, cut into wedges with cream.

QUIZ ANSWERS

1. In 1646, during the Civil War, Charles I was held prisoner for one night at the Red Hall in Upper Head Row. One of the stories surrounding the king's short stay in Leeds concerns John Harrison, a wealthy local man. On hearing that the king was being held in Leeds, Harrison asked permission to meet him and present him with a tankard of ale. The king accepted Harrison's offer, and on opening the lid of the tankard he found it full of golden guineas, which 'his Majesty did, with much celerity, hasten to secrete about his royal person'.

2. One feature of the housing that was built for the industrial workers of Leeds was the style of houses known as blind-backs, which had no rear windows or doors. From the end elevation they looked like a house that had been cut in half with one half pulled down. Some blind-backs were built up against factory walls, and others were built so that they looked like ordinary houses from the outside, with a central porch. In fact these were two blind-backs, each consisting of four single-room houses, probably accommodating 30 or more people.

3. In March 1809 Mary Bateman, a resident of Leeds, was tried and found guilty of fraud and murder, and was executed at York. Her body was then taken to the General Infirmary at Leeds where it was exhibited at a charge of 3 pence per head. Over 2,500 people paid to see the body. Later it was dissected and, following an old Yorkshire custom, her skin was tanned and distributed in small pieces to those who applied.

4. In 1925 Leeds University launched an appeal for £500,000 to build a new medical school, departmental buildings, library and student union. Lord Brotherton gave £100,000 to the appeal, and also donated his private collection of rare books. The Brotherton Library now contains over 500,000 volumes.

5. Dr Walter Farquhar Hook (Bishop of Leeds, portrayed as a fiery preacher); James Watt (inventor); Joseph Priestley (born near Leeds, he was a scientist who made important discoveries about oxygen, and is portrayed with a magnifying glass and a pestle and mortar); and John Harrison, the 17th-century merchant who gave Charles I his golden guineas.

6. Marks & Spencer: the Lithuanian immigrant Michael Marks opened his first Penny Bazaar stall in Leeds in 1884, selling buttons, wool, socks and stockings, before moving to Skipton where he co-founded Marks & Spencer with Tom Spencer.

7. She represents Circe, a figure from Greek mythology. She was the daughter of the sun, and a sorceress best known for her ability to turn men into animals. When Odysseus and his men landed on her island on their long journey home from the siege of Troy, she bewitched them and turned the crew into swine. However, Circe's spells had no effect on Odysseus, as he had earlier been given a herb of protection by Hermes to resist her power. Realising she had no power over Odysseus, Circe lifted the spell from the crew, and welcomed them to her home. They stayed there for a year before continuing their journey, and Circe bore Odysseus a son.

8. 'The Knightsbridge of the North'.

9. Leeds was in the area of the old British/Celtic kingdom of Elmet, which survived for some time even after the coming of the Anglo-Saxons.

10. In the 1930s an amnesty on weapons kept as mementos after the First World War produced 300 firearms, which were sunk in the lake in Roundhay Park during the darkest nights. A few years ago the lake was drained for maintenance, and the police patrolled the area to prevent the weapons being retrieved.

BOAR LANE c1965 L28146

BRIGGATE c1965 L28089

FRANCIS FRITH

PIONEER VICTORIAN PHOTOGRAPHER

Francis Frith, founder of the world-famous photographic archive, was a complex and multi-talented man. A devout Quaker and a highly successful Victorian businessman, he was philosophical by nature and pioneering in outlook. By 1855 he had already established a wholesale grocery business in Liverpool, and sold it for the astonishing sum of £200,000, which is the equivalent today of over £15,000,000. Now in his thirties, and captivated by the new science of photography, Frith set out on a series of pioneering journeys up the Nile and to the Near East.

INTRIGUE AND EXPLORATION

He was the first photographer to venture beyond the sixth cataract of the Nile. Africa was still the mysterious 'Dark Continent', and Stanley and Livingstone's historic meeting was a decade into the future. The conditions for picture taking confound belief. He laboured for hours in his wicker dark-room in the sweltering heat of the desert, while the volatile chemicals fizzed dangerously in their trays. Back in London he exhibited his photographs and was 'rapturously cheered' by members of the Royal Society. His reputation as a photographer was made overnight.

VENTURE OF A LIFE-TIME

By the 1870s the railways had threaded their way across the country, and Bank Holidays and half-day Saturdays had been made obligatory by Act of Parliament. All of a sudden the working man and his family were able to enjoy days out, take holidays, and see a little more of the world.

With typical business acumen, Francis Frith foresaw that these new tourists would enjoy having souvenirs to commemorate their days out. For the next thirty years he travelled the country by train and by pony and trap, producing fine photographs of seaside resorts and beauty spots that were keenly bought by millions of Victorians. These prints were painstakingly pasted into family albums and pored over during the dark nights of winter, rekindling precious memories of summer excursions. Frith's studio was soon supplying retail shops all over the country, and by 1890 F Frith & Co had become the greatest specialist photographic publishing company in the world, with over 2,000 sales outlets, and pioneered the picture postcard.

FRANCIS FRITH'S LEGACY

Francis Frith had died in 1898 at his villa in Cannes, his great project still growing. By 1970 the archive he created contained over a third of a million pictures showing 7,000 British towns and villages.

Frith's legacy to us today is of immense significance and value, for the magnificent archive of evocative photographs he created provides a unique record of change in the cities, towns and villages throughout Britain over a century and more. Frith and his fellow studio photographers revisited locations many times down the years to update their views, compiling for us an enthralling and colourful pageant of British life and character.

We are fortunate that Frith was dedicated to recording the minutiae of everyday life. For it is this sheer wealth of visual data, the painstaking chronicle of changes in dress, transport, street layouts, buildings, housing and landscape that captivates us so much today, offering us a powerful link with the past and with the lives of our ancestors.

Computers have now made it possible for Frith's many thousands of images to be accessed almost instantly. The archive offers every one of us an opportunity to examine the places where we and our families have lived and worked down the years. Its images, depicting our shared past, are now bringing pleasure and enlightenment to millions around the world a century and more after his death.

For further information visit: www.francisfrith.com

INTERIOR DECORATION

Frith's photographs can be seen framed and as giant wall murals in thousands of pubs, restaurants, hotels, banks, retail stores and other public buildings throughout Britain. These provide interesting and attractive décor, generating strong local interest and acting as a powerful reminder of gentler days in our increasingly busy and frenetic world.

FRITH PRODUCTS

All Frith photographs are available as prints and posters in a variety of different sizes and styles. In the UK we also offer a range of other gift and stationery products illustrated with Frith photographs, although many of these are not available for delivery outside the UK – see our web site for more information on the products available for delivery in your country.

THE INTERNET

Over 100,000 photographs of Britain can be viewed and purchased on the Frith web site. The web site also includes memories and reminiscences contributed by our customers, who have personal knowledge of localities and of the people and properties depicted in Frith photographs. If you wish to learn more about a specific town or village you may find these reminiscences fascinating to browse. Why not add your own comments if you think they would be of interest to others? See **www.francisfrith.com**

PLEASE HELP US BRING FRITH'S PHOTOGRAPHS TO LIFE

Our authors do their best to recount the history of the places they write about. They give insights into how particular towns and villages developed, they describe the architecture of streets and buildings, and they discuss the lives of famous people who lived there. But however knowledgeable our authors are, the story they tell is necessarily incomplete.

Frith's photographs are so much more than plain historical documents. They are living proofs of the flow of human life down the generations. They show real people at real moments in history; and each of those people is the son or daughter of someone, the brother or sister, aunt or uncle, grandfather or grandmother of someone else. All of them lived, worked and played in the streets depicted in Frith's photographs.

We would be grateful if you would give us your insights into the places shown in our photographs: the streets and buildings, the shops, businesses and industries. Post your memories of life in those streets on the Frith website: what it was like growing up there, who ran the local shop and what shopping was like years ago; if your workplace is shown tell us about your working day and what the building is used for now. Read other visitors' memories and reconnect with your shared local history and heritage. With your help more and more Frith photographs can be brought to life, and vital memories preserved for posterity, and for the benefit of historians in the future.

Wherever possible, we will try to include some of your comments in future editions of our books. Moreover, if you spot errors in dates, titles or other facts, please let us know, because our archive records are not always completely accurate—they rely on 140 years of human endeavour and hand-compiled records. You can email us using the contact form on the website.

Thank you!

For further information, trade, or author enquiries
please contact us at the address below:

**The Francis Frith Collection, Frith's Barn, Teffont,
Salisbury, Wiltshire, England SP3 5QP.**
Tel: +44 (0)1722 716 376 Fax: +44 (0)1722 716 881
e-mail: sales@francisfrith.co.uk **www.francisfrith.com**